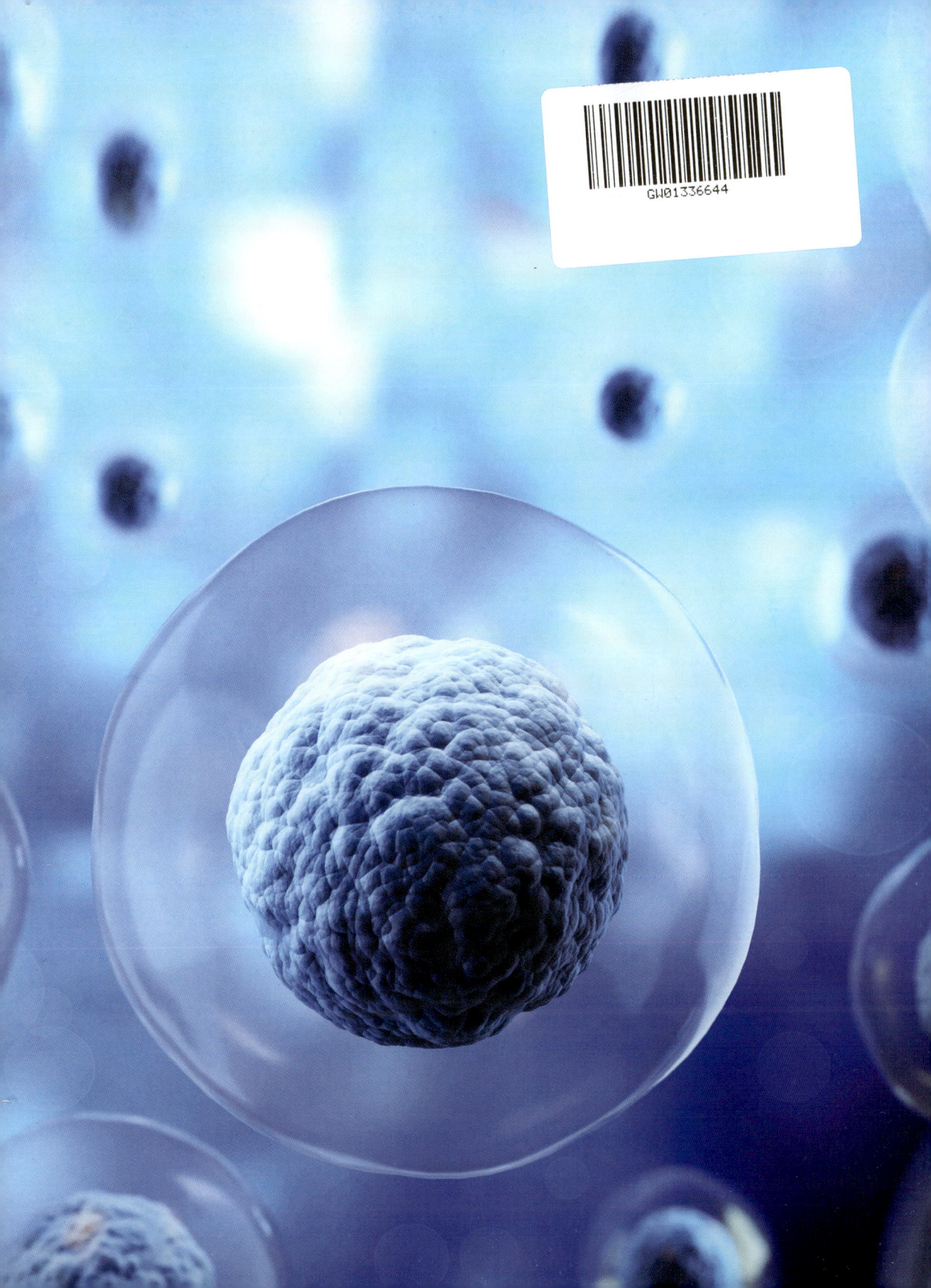

First published in 2024 by HarperCollins *Children's Books*
An imprint of HarperCollins *Publishers* India
4th Floor, Tower A, Building No. 10, DLF Cyber City,
DLF Phase II, Gurugram, Haryana – 122002
www.harpercollins.co.in

2 4 6 8 10 9 7 5 3 1

Text copyright © HarperCollins *Publishers* India 2024

P-ISBN: 978-93-6569-473-4
E-ISBN: 978-93-6569-485-7

All rights reserved. No part of this publication may be reproduced,
stored in a retrieval system, or transmitted, in any form or by any means,
electronic, mechanical, photocopying, recording or otherwise,
without the prior permission of the publishers.

While every effort has been made to ensure that the most significant of India's achievements in science are covered in the book, and that the facts presented, verified to the extent possible, are accurate and error-free, the publishers are not in any way liable for any gaps or errors that might have crept in.

Design, inside illustrations, poster and cover: Clouds Studio
Text compilation and editing: Seetha Natesh
Cover photos: Shutterstock—Orawan Pattarawimonchai, Anusorn Nakdee

Printed and bound at
Nutech Print Services - India

THE INDIA SERIES

INDIA IN SCIENCE

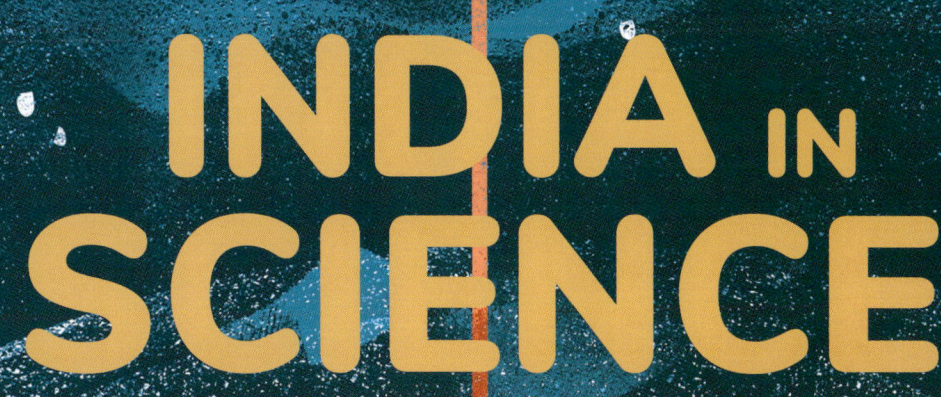

HCCB
HARPERCOLLINS
CHILDREN'S BOOKS

CONTENTS

ARCHITECTURE	6
ASTRONOMY	8
CVR Vishveshwara	10
Manali Kallat Vainu Bappu	12
Meghnad Saha	14
Mysore Rockets	16
Vikram Sarabhai	18
BOTANY	20
Benjamin Peary Pal	22
Birbal Sahni	24
Jagadish Chandra Bose	26
Janaki Ammal	28
CHEMISTRY	
Asima Chatterjee	30
CNR Rao	32
Prafulla Chandra Ray	34
GEOLOGY	
DN Wadia	36
MADE IN INDIA	38
Dyes and Mordants	40
Ink and paper	42

M Visvesvaraya — 44
PC Mahalonobis — 46
Shampoo — 48

METALLURGY — 50

QUANTUM PHYSICS — 52
GN Ramachandran — 54
Homi J Bhabha — 56
The Raman Effect — 58

WILDLIFE BIOLOGY
Counting Cats — 60
Salim Ali — 62

TRADITIONAL MEDICINE — 64
Kala Azar — 66
Ram Nath Chopra — 68
How India Became the World's Vaccine Hub — 70

Nobel Gallery — 72
Premier Science Institutions in India — 74
Science Activities — 76

ARCHITECTURE

Binding for centuries: How does lime mortar hold India's monuments together?

It's hard to imagine life without concrete. Since its birth in 1824, concrete has conquered the world. It became popular in the 1940s, when the West needed an affordable way to build anew after the devastation caused by the Second World War. In India, its popularity took off when multi-storey buildings began to be built in the 1960s and 70s. Though its usefulness is undeniable, concrete generates a huge amount of carbon dioxide. If the cement industry were a country, it would be the third largest emitter in the world, after China and the US. Concrete towers have given a uniform look to cities, wiping out local architectural traditions and knowledge. Before concrete came along, much of the world depended on lime mortar. It was used in Egypt for plastering the pyramids, and in India, as far back as the Indus Valley period. A staple in Indian architectural traditions for both binding material and coating the surface through plastering and decorating, lime mortar has been used in temples, mausoleums and forts across the country.

Longlasting Lime
The Taj Mahal, the Bibi ka Maqbara, havelis in Rajasthan's Shekhawati district, the Sanchi Stupa were all built with lime mortar.

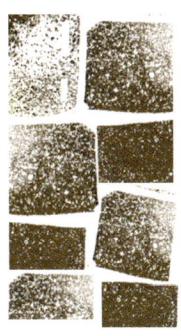

An Ancient Recipe

Locally available forms of calcium carbonate—limestone, chalk, seashells— were crushed and heated to about 900°C, converting it to calcium oxide (quicklime). When treated with water, this converts to a fine powder of calcium hydroxide (slaked lime). This was mixed with sand to prescribed proportions for a basic mortar. The other ingredients depended on local climate and the specific use of the mortar. For instance, sugar compounds such as jaggery make the mortar waterproof; jute fibres increase the strength and reduce wear and tear; fenugreek seeds, fruit pulp improve its workability while eggshells impart a sheen for decorative plastering.

The elasticity of lime mortar allows it to be moulded to the artist's will.

HAIR SPA

In ancient Rome, around 753BCE - 535CE, women coloured their hair to a light red hue with unslaked lime.

A Green Solution

Lime allows structures to 'breathe', letting moisture evaporate. On the other hand, cement seals it inside, leading to seepage. Softer than cement, lime leaves the brickwork flexible, allowing it to adapt to shifting ground conditions. This is why buildings made with lime mortar have lasted centuries. It is also far more environment friendly, producing far less carbon dioxide than cement. Recognizing these advantages, modern scientists, engineers and architects have started working with the few skilled artisans who can teach them how to work with lime plaster, paving the way for a world that's more green, less grey.

ASTRONOMY

The mysteries of the universe teased out by ancient Indians

The sun, moon and stars were the earliest gods of people. For the first farmer-settlers, whose lives depended on these heavenly bodies, knowledge of when the rains would arrive, or when the sun or moon would set, was crucial. This is how astronomy (the study of heavenly bodies) and astrology (the study of the stars to predict people's fates) were born.

In India, the first known records of astronomy are found in the Rigveda (1700 – 1100BCE). The earliest astronomical text, the *Vedanga Jyotisha* (1000BCE), attributed to Lagadha, gives rules for empirical observations and details important aspects of time. The pre-common era in India saw many breakthroughs, and from the 4th century BCE, astronomy was enriched by interactions between the Indians, Greeks, Babylonians and Persians.

First Watch
One of the earliest timekeeping devices, a sundial tells time by the position of the sun in the sky.

Ancient Astronomers

By the 5th century, Indian astronomy had made great strides. Aryabhata's ideas were influential for centuries, many valid even today. He noted that a day begins at midnight, that the earth is a sphere and that it spins on its own axis, which is why the sky appears to be in motion, among other things. Other astronomers such as Varahamihira proposed the idea of gravity, noting the existence of a force that held objects in place.

Aryabhata's Aryabhatiya offers many ideas central to modern astronomy.

The Medieval Period

Later astronomers such as Brahmagupta, Bhaskara I and Lalla proposed methods for calculating eclipses, the position of heavenly bodies over time, and studied the motion of the earth, among other things. Such calculations required reliable instruments, and those such as the gnomon, the clepsydra, as well as the seamless celestial globe are credited to Indian ingenuity.

The Jantar Mantar at Jaipur, with the world's largest stone sundial, has outlived its purpose and is now only a tourist attraction.

By the time Maharaja Jai Singh II of Amber (1688 – 1743) built the Jantar Mantar observatories, Indian traditions had stagnated and given way to those of the West. In 1777 Mir Muhammad Hussain, who had returned from England, argued the existence of multiple universes each with their own planets and stars, proof of god's power. This idea resembles the modern concept of a galaxy. From hereon, Indian astronomers would find fame only in the 20th century.

AN ABIDING MYSTERY

Ancient Indian astrologers made startling discoveries about the universe centuries before the invention of the telescope in the 1600s in The Netherlands.

The Black Hole Man of India

CHANNAPATTANA VENKATA RAMAYYA VISHVESHWARA

6 March 1938 – 16 January 2017

Fellow, Indian Academy of Sciences, Bangalore (1977)

Vishveshwara had a great sense of humour and would make cartoons that reflected or parodied scientific theories or events.

> "Black holes at that time were not a source of anything ... not even income!"

C V Vishveshwara is the man who described black holes, astronomical objects with such strong gravity that they pull everything, including light, into them. He proposed a structure for black holes, proved that they would be stable after they are formed and described the vibration pattern of their gravitational waves. He did this in 1970, even before there was proof of their existence, using logic and current scientific theories! Nearly fifty years later, on 16 October 2017, scientists announced the first ever detection of gravitational waves, and their pattern was as Vishveshwara had predicted! Though he worked with complex subjects, Vishveshwara excelled in communicating science in an easy and accessible manner, inspiring generations to a career in science.

- Shaped our knowledge of black holes through his work and encouraged research in physics, particularly on black holes, in India.
- Popularized science through his jargon-free writing and cartoons.
- Designed interactive and engaging exhibits and movies to communicate scientific concepts in an accessible way to even the very young.
- Created opportunities for collaboration between Indian and international researchers in the field.
- Initiated a number of science education programmes for children where the emphasis was on communicating deep and complex ideas in an accessible manner.

MK Vainu Bappu had always been fascinated by the skies. His training started early—as a child, he would accompany his father, an astronomer, to the Nizamiah Observatory, Hyderabad. He was keen to pursue a degree in astronomy, but there were no such courses in India, and he did not have enough money to go abroad. Fortunately, fate took matter into its hands. Renowned astronomer Harlow Shapley, who was visiting Hyderabad, met Bappu and was immediately impressed. The rest is history. Bappu received a scholarship, enrolled at Harvard University, and went on to prove that Shapley's trust in him was well placed. He would make great contributions to astronomy, including discovering a comet, furthering our understanding of stars and even leading the prestigious International Astronomical Union, the only Indian to do so.

Discovered the Wilson-Bappu effect, which made an important observation on the light that Wolf-Rayet stars gave off, in collaboration with his colleague Colin Wilson. Now known as the Wilson-Bappu effect, it helps determine the distance of remote stars and study their atmospheres.

Set up observatories in Nainital and Kavalur, and headed the Kodaikanal Observatory.

Was the founder-director of the Indian Institute of Astrophysics, Bangalore.

Discovered the Bappu-Bok-Newkirk comet with colleagues Bart Bok and Gordon Newkirk in 1949. He's the only Indian with a comet named after him.

Meghnad Saha's greatest contribution was to help shape astronomy into an exact and predictive science. In 1919, Saha read a paper on thermal ionization (a process where atoms lose electrons on heating) that sparked an idea—and resolved a problem that had been around for ages. Since the mid-19th century, stars had been grouped according to their spectra (thin black lines that appeared when starlight was passed through a prism). Saha realized that when scientists did this, they were actually grouping stars according to their temperature. With his equation on thermal ionization, astronomers could gather other information about stars, such as their actual temperature and the elements they contained. Nearly all later work in this field has been influenced by Saha's research.

Explained phenomena such as comet tails; initiated research on cosmic rays, the ionosphere and geophysics.

Promoted science and scientific societies, including the Institute of Nuclear Physics, National Academy of Science and Indian Institute of Science.

Invented an instrument to measure the weight and pressure of solar rays.

Was the chief architect of river planning in India and prepared the initial plan for the Damodar Valley Project.

MYSORE ROCKETS

The weapon that fuelled the idea of space travel

Tipu Sultan, the ruler of Mysore, was a force to reckon with. He cost the British four wars over three decades (1767–99) to bring his kingdom under their rule. Only a brilliant military strategist could have held off the British for so long, and Tipu's daring tactics and well equipped army sent shivers up the collective British spine. He also had a devastating weapon ...

The Flying Plague

Though Tipu didn't invent the rocket (they had been in use since the 13th century), he overhauled the technology, creating a weapon that wreaked such havoc that the British called it the 'Flying Plague'. His father Haider Ali had made the rocket deadlier by packing the wood/cardboard body with explosives; Tipu revamped the design by encasing the explosives in iron tubes. The iron casing made these rockets more powerful in terms of their range— 2.4km, the farthest at the time—as well as impact. Tipu then had these fastened to swords or bamboo poles to provide stability and improve accuracy.

Small but Deadly
The Mysore rockets were far deadlier than the British cannons— and were much easier to transport.

ANOTHER CASUALTY OF WAR
Noor Inayat Khan, a distant descendant of Tipu Sultan, worked with the British as a spy during the Second World War. She was caught and executed at the Dachau concentration camp in Germany in 1944.

The Best in Business
These precursors of the modern rocket helped Tipu win many wars and was far more devastating than any other existing weapon. Well aware of their importance to his defence, he set up research centres that worked on improving the iron casing, accuracy, range and impact of the rockets. He also experimented with rockets of different sizes and weights to hit targets at varying distances and elevations.

Portrait of Tipu Sultan, circa 1790–1800

Firing Up the World—and Beyond
In 1799, the British finally conquered Mysore. They took over Srirangapatna, the capital, then seized Tipu's armoury and sent a few of his rockets to the English inventor William Congreve. Based on these specimens, Congreve developed similar rockets that were used in 1812 against the USA and helped defeat Napoleon at Waterloo in 1815. These 'Congreve rockets' fired the imagination of many, and by the end of the 19th century, people were studying the fundamental science behind rocketry and considering the possibility of space travel. Tipu's innovation had a far-reaching impact, one that NASA certainly recognizes. Its Wallops Flight Facility displays a painting of the Mysore rockets being fired at the British.

A painting depicting the Battle of Guntur (1790) and the devastation the British suffered from the rockets

Architect of India's Space Programme

VIKRAM SARABHAI

12 August 1919 – 30 December 1971

Padma Bhushan (1966), Padma Vibhushan (1972), Vice President, Fourth UN Conference on 'Peaceful Uses of Atomic Energy' (1971)

Both Sarabhai and Homi Bhabha died suddenly, prompting conspiracy theories that they were assassinated by US agents because of their genius in nuclear technology.

Furthered our understanding of cosmic rays, energy particles that reach the Earth from outer space, through his research.

"We look down on our scientists if they engage in outside consultation. We implicitly promote the ivory tower."

Vikram Sarabhai's name is synonymous with India's space programme. He initiated space research in India and furthered the country's nuclear programme. Recognizing the enormous potential of space science to impact national development, he started programmes for communication, weather forecasting and exploring natural resources through satellites. All these programmes had an impact on the daily life of all Indians. The International Astronomical Union recognized his contributions to space research by naming a lunar crater after him.

- Initiated space research in India and established premier facilities such as the Physical Research Lab and the Indian Space Research Organisation.

- Initiated space programmes to beam lessons to remote villages through satellite communication, proposed the development of satellite based weather and natural disaster forecasts.

- Helped establish India's nuclear power plants, laid the foundation for local development of nuclear technology for defence and chaired the Atomic Energy Commission.

- Set up the nation's first rocket launching station at Thumba and a project to create and launch an Indian satellite.

- Set up a number of institutions in non-science fields including the Operations Research Group—the first market research company in the country—the Indian Institute of Management Ahmedabad and the Ahmedabad Textile Industry's Research Association.

BOTANY

Ancient India was highly advanced in plant science

The history of botany is as old as humans, perhaps older. Knowing what to eat and what *not* to, what would help heal cuts and wounds—these were key to survival.

Advances in Botany

In India, the earliest knowledge of plants is in the Rigveda (1500 – 1200BCE), which mentions the action of light on the process and storage of energy. By the time of the Atharvaveda (1000–900BCE), botany was flourishing. The Atharvaveda extensively classifies plants by colour, character, habitat and use. An advanced knowledge of plants is seen in technical literature like the *Charaka* and *Sushruta Samhitas*, Kautilya's *Artha-sastra*, Patanjali's *Mahabhasya*, *Krishi-Parashara* and Varahmihira's *Brhat Samhita*; encyclopaedia like the *Medini nighantu* and Amarasimha's *Amarakosa*; lay literature such as plays by Kalidasa, Magha and Bhavabhuti; and religious texts such as the Upanishads, the Mahabharata and the Ramayana.

Many of these texts reveal knowledge of plant diseases and their treatment; of genders in plants and of various methods of plant reproduction such as from fruit, seeds, roots, shoots, leaves, cuttings and even grafts. Some even assert that plants are capable of sensations such as pleasure and pain, an idea that JC Bose, another Indian, would prove many centuries later.

The Father of Indian Botany

The most ancient work solely on botany is Parashara's *Vrikshayurveda* (BCE 1st century – 1st century CE). This treatise was discovered as recently as the 20th century and describes concepts such as photosynthesis; kinds of seeds; seed formation, starting from the very nucleus; plant cells and their structure and the inner tissues that transport water and nutrients throughout the plants. These concepts only came to light in western science in the 17th century, after the invention of the microscope in 1590. In fact, Parashara concedes that these microscopic structures are not visible to the naked eye. So how did he study them? Though there has been considerable speculation on whether ancient Indians used microscope-like instruments, we have no concrete answers so far. Who knows if the answers lie hidden in yet another undiscovered text?

A Close-up
Robert Hooke discovered cells when he studied cork under a microscope in 1665. This is a drawing of what he saw, published in his *Micrographia*.

Now cultivated across the world, the banana is native to India and is mentioned in several ancient Indian texts.

THE FATHER OF BOTANY

The history of science—like all histories—has been written by the West. Thus, Theophrastus (c. 371–287 BCE) is generally regarded as the father of botany. A disciple of Aristotle, Theophrastus wrote influential books on botany and is credited with promoting the study of plants.

India's Foremost Agricultural Scientist

BENJAMIN PEARY PAL

26 May 1906 – 14 September 1989

S. Ramanujan Medal (1964),
Padma Bhushan (1968),
Fellow, Royal Society (1972),
Padma Vibhushan (1987)

In the 1960s, India suffered a great food shortage that left millions starving. While trade agreements helped plug the deficit for a while, they would not be sustainable in the long term. The solution lay in breeding staple food crops that were resistant to common pests and required less water to grow. As head of the Indian Agricultural Research Institute and the first Director-General of the Indian Council of Agricultural Research, Dr BP Pal launched the first phase of the country's Green Revolution, helping transform India from a starving to a food surplus nation. In 2007, India's Department of Posts printed a commemorative stamp of Pal to honour his contribution to the country.

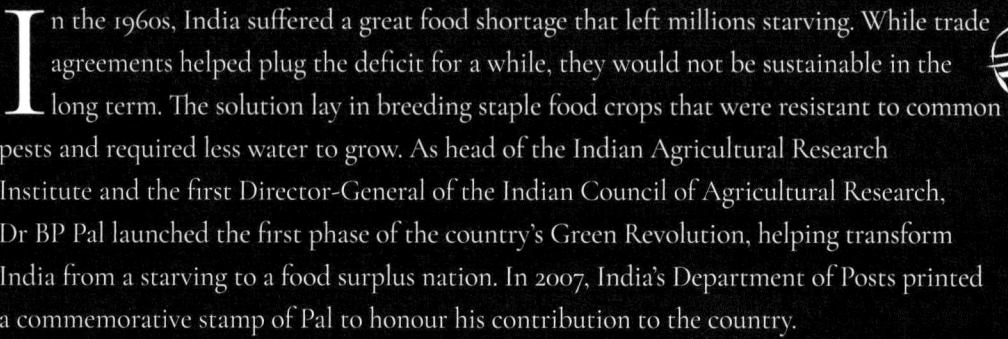

- Bred wheat varieties that were disease resistant and required less water, helping India become a food surplus nation.
- Introduced social science in his institutes to help scientists understand the actual impact of their work, a model now followed by many developing nations such as Pakistan, Bangladesh, Philippines and Nigeria.
- Introduced modern technology to breed varieties of food and cash crops such as tobacco, tomato and potato.
- Scouted for talented scientists within and outside India to collaborate with, building a number of institutions to promote agricultural research.
- Encouraged research in animal husbandry and fisheries to strengthen the Green Revolution.

"Under Dr Pal's leadership ... the agronomic research on wheat in India equalled the best in the world. He was truly the architect of India's Green Revolution."
NORMAN BORLAUG

Pal was a rose breeder of distinction and created several new varieties of the flower. He helped set up the rose garden in Chandigarh.

Chaired the first National Committee on Environmental Protection and Coordination and was a vocal supporter of conservation.

Founder of Paleobotany in India

BIRBAL SAHNI

14 November 1891 – 10 April 1949

Fellow of the Royal Society (1936), General President, Indian Science Congress (1940), President, Indian National Science Academy (1937–1939 and 1943–1944)

Right from a very young age, Birbal Sahni was interested in the building blocks of paleobotany, the study of fossil plants. As a child, he had painstakingly built an impressive collection of plants and rocks over trips through the Himalayas. These trips perhaps taught him to think in terms of the big picture and connect what are generally distinct, independent fields of study—botany, geology and history. While all three fields owe him a great debt, he is most widely recognized as the father of paleobotany in India. His championship of paleobotany has ensured research in the field beyond his lifetime.

His research, particularly on ancient plants and fossils, furthered knowledge not only in botany, but also in geology and history. These include the theory of continental drift, the age of the Deccan Intertrappean Beds in Andhra Pradesh and the Salt Range hills in Pakistan. He also described the process of coin minting in the ancient Indian kingdom of Yaudheya.

Systematized paleobotany into an organized field in India and founded the Institute of Paleobotany in Lucknow, the only organization in the world dedicated to the study of the subject. This was renamed the Birbal Sahni Institute of Paleobotany after his death.

Inspired interest in botany and geology (and sciences in general) through his teaching and research. His reputation as a great teacher attracted students from all over the country and helped paleobotany flourish.

"The aim of [the palaeobotanist and archaeologist] is historical: the interpretation and reconstruction of the past."

Birbal Sahni's popularity with the youth extended to the very young as well. Fondly called the tamashewala uncle by nieces and nephews, he would entertain them for hours with his monkey hand-puppet, Gippy.

Father of Wireless Communication

JAGADISH CHANDRA BOSE

30 November 1858 – 23 November 1937

Fellow of the Royal Society (1920), Member of the Vienna Academy of Sciences (1928), Fellow of the Indian National Science Academy, Member of Finnish Society of Sciences and Letters (1929)

A crater on the moon is named in Bose's honour, in recognition of his work on wireless communication.

> *"The true laboratory is the mind, where behind illusions we uncover the laws of truth."*

Undoubtedly among the greatest Indian scientists, JC Bose was a polymath whose contributions span virtually the whole spectrum of knowledge, from physics to archaeology, botany, radio science and literature. Working from a tiny workshop fitted out at his own expense at Kolkata's Presidency College (where he was denied a lab because of his race), his breakthrough discoveries and inventions made waves throughout the science world. He could have become a rich man had he patented even a few of these devices, but he chose not to do so, believing that knowledge should be freely available to all.

- Proved that plants respond to external stimuli such as heat, pain and music, thus establishing that plants have life, a fundamental fact now taught all over in schools.

- Earned the moniker 'Acharya' or expert teacher with his extremely popular physics lessons, where he emphasized the importance of questioning everything, including textbooks.

- Made the first public demonstration of wireless technology, the basis of modern communication, in 1895, two years before Marconi: He remotely rang an electric bell and ignited a small charge of gunpowder using microwaves, a technology no one else had used so far.

- Wrote the short stories *Niruddesher Kahini (The Story of the Missing One, 1896)* and *Palatak Tuphan (Runaway Cyclone, 1921)*, early examples of science fiction in India, making him the father of Bengali science fiction.

Mother of Modern Botany in India

JANAKI AMMAL
4 November 1897 – 7 February 1984

First Indian woman to receive a PhD in botany in the US, Fellow of the Indian Academy of Sciences (1935), Fellow of the Indian National Science Academy (1957), Padma Shri (1977)

Dr Edavaleth Kakkat Janaki Ammal was the exception to the norm in more ways than one. At a time when the national literacy rate for women was less than 1 per cent, she chose to pursue a PhD, on a scholarship. When the only way forward for women was to get married, she chose to be single. She was singled out for her caste and gender, but she ploughed through, earning herself a grand reputation as a botanist across the globe.

- Developed several hybrid crop species still grown today, including varieties of sweet sugarcane that made India self-sufficient in sugarcane production.

- Hired as a cytologist at the prestigious Royal Horticultural Society, she became its first salaried woman staff member.

- Wrote the seminal *Chromosome Atlas of Cultivated Plants* with geneticist Cyril Darlington. Unlike atlases that focused on botanical classification, this atlas recorded the chromosome number of about 100,000 plants, and examined the breeding and evolutionary patterns of botanical groups.

- Headed the prestigious Central Botanical Laboratory in Lucknow and reorganized the Botanical Survey of India to improve the botanical base of Indian agriculture.

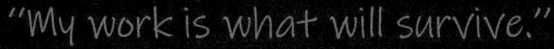

"My work is what will survive."

Janaki Ammal's name lives on in the Magnolia kobus Janaki Ammal, a cross-bred variety of magnolia that she helped create. This variety, with its pure white blooms, is highly prized and found in very few nurseries in Europe.

Championed the preservation and study of India's indigenous plants and of indigenous approaches to the environment.

First Woman to Earn a Doctorate from an Indian University

ASIMA CHATTERJEE

23 September 1917 – 22 November 2006

Fellow of the Indian National Science Academy (1960), Padma Bhushan (1975), Rajya Sabha Member (1982–90)

Chatterjee won the Shanti Swarup Bhatnagar Prize in 1961. She was the first woman to receive India's most prestigious science award.

The first woman to earn a PhD in India, Asima Chatterjee deserves recognition for just that achievement. But this was just the beginning of a career that had many notables. Chatterjee was a pioneer in organic chemistry whose work helped in the treatment of a variety of diseases, notably malaria, epilepsy and cancer, and focused on chemical compounds produced by plants native to the Indian subcontinent. She was the first woman general president of the Indian Science Congress Association and won several prestigious awards, including the SS Bhatnagar award, the CV Raman award and the PC Ray award.

Developed Ayush-56, an antiepileptic drug, along with several antimalarial drugs that have been patented and have treated several thousands of people.

Wrote extensively on medicinal plants of the Indian subcontinent and published close to 400 papers. Her work has been extensively cited and been included in several textbooks.

Worked on compounds from the Madagascar periwinkle plant, called vinca alkaloids, and helped develop drugs used in chemotherapy treatment.

Founded the department of chemistry at Lady Brabourne College, Calcutta University.

"I wish to work as long as I live."

A Giant in the World of Chemistry

CNR RAO
b. 30 June 1934

Shanti Swarup Bhatnagar Prize for Science and Technology (1968), India Science Award (2004), Dan David Prize (2005), Bharat Ratna (2014)

As Scientific Advisor to the Prime Minister of India, guided national policies on science.

Rao was eleven years old when a school visit by Nobel laureate and physicist CV Raman inspired him to take up science.

Hailed as the man who has won all the prizes in his field except the Nobel, CNR Rao is one of the world's foremost names in materials chemistry, the science which studies, designs, creates and analyzes new forms of matter. He has written over 1,500 papers and 50 books and with over 44,000 citations, is one of the most cited chemists in the world. His research in several areas of chemistry, from superconductors to artificial photosynthesis, has led to greater knowledge of those subjects.

Nurtured and built many reputed science institutions, including IIT Kanpur, Indian Institute of Science, Bengaluru, Jawaharlal Nehru Institute for Advanced Research, Bengaluru, as well as the Indian Institutes of Science Education and Research.

Contributed extensively to nanoscience (the study of materials on an ultra-small scale) and nanotechnology.

His work on metal oxide compounds led to greater understanding and study of that field.

Known for his research on superconductors (materials that conduct electricity with no resistance) and their chemical properties, graphene and artificial photosynthesis.

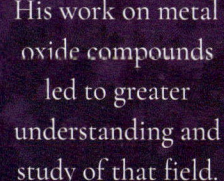

"... the best way to classify science is as ... science that has already been applied and science yet to be applied."

> "A government ... which cannot spare a farthing for laboratories, should forfeit the title of a civilized government."

Scientist, writer, entrepreneur, but above all a patriot, Sir PC Ray devoted his life to his country. He put his knowledge of chemistry to public benefit in various ways. He set up the Bengal Chemicals and Pharmaceuticals Works, the first Indian factory to manufacture affordable medicines for its people, using indigenous technology, skill and raw materials. He published articles in chemistry in popular Bengali magazines, believing knowledge should be accessible to people. He was also a renowned chemist who opened up an entirely new area of study with his research.

Discovered the compound mercurous nitrite, which spawned a whole new field of research.

Wrote *The History of Hindu Chemistry*, which helped the West appreciate the scientific prowess of ancient and medieval India in chemistry and gave Indians a sense of pride in their own scientific heritage.

Published over 150 papers, a few with collaborators, in reputed journals across the world.

Founded Bengal Chemicals and Pharmaceuticals Works with his student Amulyacharan Bose. Encouraged other homegrown industries that made products that Indians could afford.

Believed in making science accessible. He wrote on science in popular magazines and his college lectures (where the emphasis was more on 'show' than 'tell') were extremely popular.

Founded the Indian Chemical Society, which published the *Journal of the Indian Chemical Society*, India's first research journal.

India's First National Professor in Geology
DN WADIA
23 October 1883 – 15 June 1969

Fellow of the Royal Academy of Sciences (1957), Back Award (1934), Lyell Medal (1943), Padma Bhushan (1958)

Wrote the monumental *The Geology of India* to offer students an up-to-date resource on the subject, and which is studied across the world even today.

Wadia's interest in the earth sciences was sparked by his brother Munchershaw Wadia, who was an educationist in the princely state of Baroda.

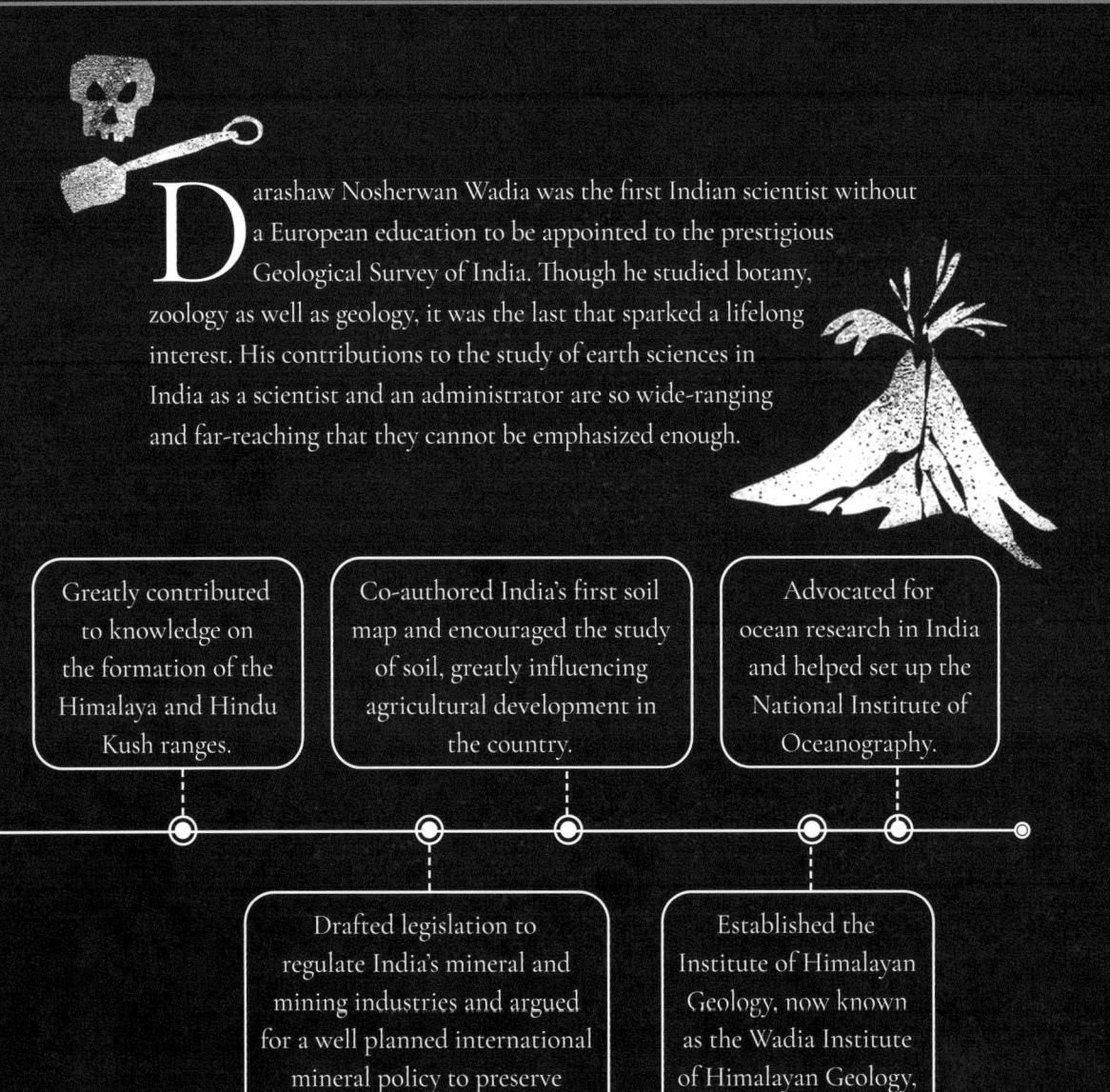

Darashaw Nosherwan Wadia was the first Indian scientist without a European education to be appointed to the prestigious Geological Survey of India. Though he studied botany, zoology as well as geology, it was the last that sparked a lifelong interest. His contributions to the study of earth sciences in India as a scientist and an administrator are so wide-ranging and far-reaching that they cannot be emphasized enough.

- Greatly contributed to knowledge on the formation of the Himalaya and Hindu Kush ranges.
- Co-authored India's first soil map and encouraged the study of soil, greatly influencing agricultural development in the country.
- Advocated for ocean research in India and helped set up the National Institute of Oceanography.
- Drafted legislation to regulate India's mineral and mining industries and argued for a well planned international mineral policy to preserve goodwill among nations.
- Established the Institute of Himalayan Geology, now known as the Wadia Institute of Himalayan Geology, in Dehradun.

"The best work is done with the least amenities."

MADE IN INDIA

India's ingenuity in engineering, seen through these everyday objects

We generally understand science as a field that examines the universe and its contents. From the distant galaxies to the minutest atom, science reveals and explains our world and the forces operating in and on it. But science is also about using those theories and applying them for practical purposes. That's what inventions are, what inventors do and what engineering is all about. Here are a few things we all use every day, and perhaps even consider as modern stuff. Actually, though, they're all rather old—and made in India at that.

Flush toilets and water drainage

Flush toilets are among the inventions most important to human health. The modern flush toilet was invented in 1596 by Sir John Harington; it had a bowl to hold excreta and a valve that released water from a tank to wash it away. But archaeologists suggest that early versions of the flush toilet were in use at least 4,000 years ago in the Indus Valley. Cities in the Indus Valley had sophisticated sanitation and water drainage systems, featuring communal toilets with running water. Individual homes had toilets with chutes that transported waste into covered street drains. All sewage was disposed of through underground drains into surrounding water bodies or into pits that were regularly cleaned.

Real or Rumoured?
Stories abound of the many kinds of ships in the Chola navy. The south Indian kingdom was even rumoured to have ships without nails though this has not been established as fact.

OTHER INDIAN INVENTIONS

Games require some serious ingenuity. Chess, ludo, snakes and ladders and carrom are a few games of Indian origin that are popular across the world.

Cotton Fabrics

Cotton was woven as far back as the Indus Valley Civilization in India and was a prized commodity across the world by 4,500BCE. A wide variety of cottons were woven on what now seems rather primitive machinery, from the coarse calico to the decorative chintz and the superfine muslin to name a few. These fabrics required different kinds of processing and weaving, and thus different machinery. Some of the notable ones include cotton 'gins' that separated seeds from the fibre and the charkha, the spinning wheel that became synonymous with the Indian Independence movement.

Hand-painted cotton fabric, or palampore

Prefabricated structures

Buildings that are built elsewhere, usually in bits and pieces, then assembled on the site are known as prefabricated buildings. They're usually assumed to be a modern invention, but similar moveable structures were in use in 16th-century India. The Mughal emperor Akbar was said to use an elaborate 'prefab' home called 'Gulalbar' while hunting. As described by his historian Arif Qandahari in 1579, it was a 'fortress' made of wood and bamboo panels, with a few interior chambers and even an upper story and balcony. The panels were joined with iron fittings, making for a solid enclosure.

Akbar on a hunting expedition

DYES AND MORDANTS

What made Indian fabric so special?

Much of India's history is interwoven with the history of its fabrics. Indian cloth, like its spices, has been prized since antiquity. Trade flourished both along land and sea routes, reaching places as distant as Egypt, China and Greece from the 2nd century BCE onwards. It was these products that Marco Polo and Vasco da Gama marvelled over, while the Dutch and the English founded their respective East India Companies with trade as their main aim.

The priest-king figurine recovered from the Indus Valley Civilization, wearing a red and blue/green robe

Colour Chemistry

So what made Indian cloth so valuable? While Indian fabrics, particularly cotton, were of superior quality, the plethora of colours they came in added to their beauty—and value. We may take coloured clothes for granted today, but dyeing fabric was a closely guarded secret, one that gave India a virtual monopoly over textiles for centuries.

Centres for Dyeing
Gujarat, Srikalahasti and Machilipatnam in Andhra Pradesh and the Tanjore region in Tamil Nadu were famed centres of artisanal dyeing.

40

Colouring cloth needs matching the chemical structure of the fibre with that of the dye. Dyes that work on protein fibres like wool or silk, for instance, may not work on cellulose fibres such as cotton. Also, some fibres may need other chemicals to help fix the dye to the cloth; these mordants would need to be chemically compatible with the dye and the fabric. And where the dye was not required, 'resists' made in various combinations of gum and mud or from wax would be added to make the cloth resistant to the dye. With dyes and resists, the possibilities in cloth designs were endless.

Stains from plant parts—berries, roots, shoots, leaves, etc.—perhaps gave the idea of dyes. Pictured here is the indigo plant, whose leaves are processed for the trademark blue.

To Dye For

Dyes, mordants and resists have been used in the subcontinent as far back as the Indus Valley Civilization (3300–1900BCE). As weaving and dyeing became full-fledged industries, different regions developed their own traditions of patterns, colours and materials, with practices staying within families. After establishing control over India, the British began to export Indian dyes and fabrics across the world. Trade was so lucrative that they forced farmers to grow cotton and indigo, the source of the indigo dye. With industrialization and the discovery of artificial dyes in 1856, the natural dyes industry in India suffered a huge setback. However, the recent emphasis on ecofriendly products has brought both cotton and the natural dyeing industries to the forefront, sparking new hope for the industry.

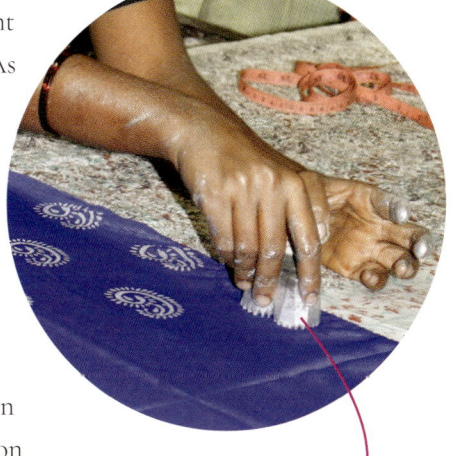

An artist block printing fabric

BACK IN HISTORY

Gandhiji's first noncooperation movement in India was the Champaran Satyagraha (1917). He organized a satyagraha in Bihar in support of farmers who were forced to grow indigo with barely any payment for it.

INK AND PAPER

Ancient and Medieval India's writing implements

Ink and paper have allowed people to read and write for centuries. These are ancient technologies whose basic formula and manufacturing process have remained the same through the ages. In India, ink, widely known as masi, was in use from the 4th century BCE while paper arrived in the 11th century CE from China. Until this time, and even as recently as the 18th century, birch bark and palm leaves were the principal writing materials in India. These days, however, they are used mainly for religious purposes.

Wanted Specialists
Writing on palm leaves required special training and instruments. Professional lipikaras used ghantams, thin metal styluses with a pointed edge, to scratch letters onto the leaves.

Tree Paper

The material depended mainly on the kind of tree that grew in that part of the country. Thus, birch bark, bhurjapatra in Sanskrit, was used mainly in the north, while palm leaves, tadapatra, were used mainly in the south and east. Both underwent processing to make them suitable for writing, but the one for palm leaves was particularly elaborate. Tender palm leaves were cut, then boiled in plain water or with paddy husk or other starch and dried in shade. The leaves were then polished with pumice stone or conch shells and cut to size. A string threaded through held the leaves together. Wooden planks slightly larger than the leaves served as covers. Treated with insecticide prepared from lacquer and minerals, they protected the leaves while keeping them flat and smooth. Such a book would often last as long as 300 years.

Once etched, the manuscripts were inked. Black, from soot; red, from iron oxide; yellow, from turmeric; and blue, from the indigo plant leaves were the popular pigments.

Pen and Ink

Brushes were used on birch bark, while a metal stylus called ghantam was needed to engrave letters onto palm leaves. As such etchings were not easily readable, masi ink would be brushed over the writing to embed it into the grooves, with any excess wiped off. This ink was carbon based, made with lamp-black or soot, which was mixed with shellac, borax, gum, which helped bind it to the paper, forming an insoluble film on leaves. Insect repellents such as camphor or citronella or other oils were also added to increase the life of the manuscripts. This 5,000-year-old recipe hasn't changed much since it was first invented and is used even today by artists for its deep colour.

PAPER SCRIPTS

Regions that used palm leaf manuscripts, such as Orissa, Karnataka, Kerala, Thailand, Indonesia and Sri Lanka, have rounded letters in their scripts. This was possibly because angular letters could tear the leaves while rounded ones could be rendered easily.

Indian sculpture; a birch bark manuscript is easily identified by the droop. A palm leaf manuscript is stiff.

The Builder of Modern India
MOKSHAGUNDAM VISVESVARAYA
15 September 1860 – 12 April 1962

Fellow of the Indian Academy of Sciences, Knight of the British Empire, Bharat Ratna (1955)

Designed a water filtration system on the riverbed to supply clean water to Sukkur, Pakistan.

Visvesvaraya's credo was 'Industrialize or perish!', while Gandhiji's was 'Industrialize and perish!' Though they had opposing views, the two respected each other.

His achievements in engineering are so staggering that three nations—India, Sri Lanka and Tanzania—celebrate his birthday as Engineer's Day. M Visvesvaraya is known for his ingenuity in conserving and harnessing water resources and designed many water supply, drainage and irrigation systems across the country. He wasn't just a whiz at applied sciences but a scholar and statesman who believed that hard work, discipline and a good education are the best tools to build a developed, industrial nation. For that reason, he was a big advocate of teaching in local languages and educating women.

- Conceptualized the 'block irrigation' system for Bombay Presidency, which supplied water to large blocks of land, reducing water wastage and increasing crop production.

- Designed an effective drainage system for Hyderabad, which would flood every time the Musi river overflowed.

- Helped in the plan to protect the sea port of Vishakhapatnam from sea erosion.

- Designed automatic barriers for dams, which would close when there was overflow of water, helping in flood control.

- Architect of the Krishna Raja Sagara Dam in Mysore, the largest reservoir in India at the time, which provided drinking water to several cities.

"It is better to work out than rust out."

Father of Modern Statistics in India

PC MAHALONOBIS
29 June 1893 – 28 June 1972

Fellow of the Indian National Science Academy (1935), Fellow of the Royal Society (1945), President, Indian Science Congress (1950), Padma Vibhushan (1968)

Though he's known as the father of modern statistics in India, PC Mahalonobis was actually a professor of physics and worked in that capacity until his retirement.

> *"[Statistics is] a new technology for increasing the efficiency of human effort in the wildest sense."*

A chance introduction to statistics via the journal *Biometrika* opened PC Mahalonobis's eyes to the possibilities of its application—and forever changed the way scientists would measure and analyze large-scale and complex phenomena. He applied statistics to subjects such as meteorology, anthropology, physics and economics and studied a vast range of topics, from crop yields, population distribution, to tea-drinking practices of middle-class Indians in Calcutta. In other words, he showed that statistics is the study of patterns and is thus useful in all areas of research. Today, it is unthinkable to work in science—or any other subject—and not use statistics.

- Laid the foundations of India's statistical infrastructure by setting up the Indian Statistical Institute, National Sample Survey Office and Central Statistical Organization. He also founded *Sankhya*, a journal on statistics.

- Analyzed sixty years' data on floods in Orissa, leading to the construction of the Hirakud dam on the Mahanadi river.

- Devised many ways of measuring, comparing and analyzing data, such as the 'Mahalonobis Distance' and the fractile graphical analysis.

- Applied statistics to economic planning and was one of the early members of the Planning Commission. His 'Mahalonobis Model' of economic growth directed the course of India's economy until the early 1990s.

SHAMPOO

The hair care regimen that India gave the world

Animals do it, birds do it, even bees do it. Grooming—keeping clean—helps keep disease-causing germs at bay and is essential to health. While animals are happy with water or saliva, humans have used specialized products to groom themselves since ancient times. In fact, the earliest reference to shampooing is from the 4th century BCE, from the writings of the Greek historian Strabo, who noted its practise in the Indian subcontinent. The traditional 'shampoo', used widely even today, is usually an extract or powder of native plant parts, such as soapberries, Indian gooseberries, hibiscus flowers, shikakai. The mixture often varies, depending on local availability of the plants. The soapberries produce a good lather when mixed with water, leaving the hair clean, while the other ingredients help keep it healthy, glossy, promote hair growth and prevent premature greying. Though science has advanced greatly since the time of this shampoo, most modern ones claim to offer these very benefits.

Hair (S)care
The *Ashtanga Hridaya*, a foundational ayurvedic text, has remedies for hairfall, greying and dandruff.

Taking the Shampoo to the World

The word 'shampoo' comes from the Sanskrit *chapyati*, which means 'to massage', and entered the English language in 1762. By 1860, it had come to mean a hair wash. The concept, like the word, came to Britain through India when Patna-born Shaikh Din Muhammad emigrated to England. He opened the first commercial shampooing bath in Brighton in 1814, advertising an 'Indian medicated vapour bath' with medicinal herbs as well as 'shampooing' with Indian oils. The business was so successful that Muhammad came to be known as 'Dr Brighton' and was appointed 'shampooing surgeon' to King George IV and William IV.

A portrait of Shaikh Din Muhammad

A Modern Invention

Soon, English hairstylists began to boil soap shavings with herbs to wash hair, a practice that spread across Europe. It was only in 1927 that the first commercially made liquid shampoo was manufactured, by Hans Schwarzkopf. The next real revolutionary idea in the industry was once again an Indian's. R Chinnikrishnan's idea of packaging shampoo in sachets made it pocket-sized, portable and affordable. More importantly, the innovation had a far wider impact, and revolutionized the fast-moving goods industry as a whole.

INDIA MADE
The first Indian brand to sell shampoos was Chik, the very same brand that would later pioneer the concept of the shampoo sachet.

Amla, the Indian gooseberry, has high amounts of Vitamin C, essential for healthy hair and skin.

METALLURGY

India was proficient in metalwork well before the Industrial Revolution

India has a rich history of metallurgy, the art and science of extracting and working with metals. Indian metalwork was extremely advanced, well ahead of many other civilizations for centuries. Here's a tour of some of its accomplishments through a few objects.

Wootz Steel

Crafted in modern-day Tamil Nadu, Wootz was a pioneering steel alloy developed as early as 400BCE. This high carbon steel was made with magnetite ore and carbon in a sealed clay crucible kept inside a charcoal furnace. (This process also gave it the distinct pattern of wavy bands reminiscent of flowing water.) It was then exported as iron cakes through the ancient and medieval world from Europe to China. The famous 'Damascus' swords that could slash a freefalling silk scarf or a block of wood with the same ease were made from Wootz.

Deadly and Dependable
Wootz steel weapons were reputed to be tough, resistant to shattering and capable of being honed to a sharp, resilient edge.

OUT-OF-PLACE (OOP) ARTEFACTS

Out-of-place (OOP) artefacts are those that seem to show a level of technical prowess unexpected in the time or place they were found. Delhi's Iron Pillar and the seamless globes are considered OOP artefacts.

Iron Pillar of Delhi

Perhaps India's most famous metal artefact, the Iron Pillar of Delhi is located within the Qutb complex, close to its more famous cousin, the Qutb Minar. Dating back to about 415CE, this pillar made of 99 per cent iron has weathered the elements for over 1,600 years, but still has not rusted, barring minor natural erosion. This kind of rust-proof iron would be hard to recreate even with today's technology. Research has shown that other large ancient Indian objects have a similar property. Other iron pillars, such as from Dhar in Madhya Pradesh, Kodachadri in Karnataka and Mount Abu in Rajasthan, establish that this was no accident, but a feat of master craftsmanship.

Portrait of Emperor Jahangir with a globe probably made by Muhammad Thattvi

Seamless Globe

Invented in Kashmir by Ali Kashmiri ibn Luqman in the reign of the Mughal emperor Akbar, the seamless celestial globe is among the most remarkable achievements in metallurgy. These metal spheres that show the relative position of the stars were made using a secret wax casting method. As the name suggests, they were made without any seams or joints, with the sphere cast as a single unit. Before they were discovered in Kashmir in the 1980s, the spheres were considered impossible to make, even with modern technology.

QUANTUM PHYSICS

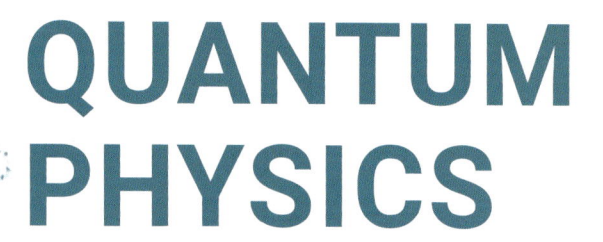

How a little-known Indian made a big splash in physics

Physics in the 20th century went through a huge shift. Classical physics, which studied visible objects and phenomena, gave way to Quantum physics, which examined the minutest bits of the universe (such as photons, electrons). As matter behaves very differently in the quantum universe, a whole new set of ideas was waiting to be discovered.

A Neat Solution

In 1900, German physicist Max Planck had proposed that the traditional idea of light as a wave may be inaccurate; that it also existed as small chunks of energy known as quanta. But to Satyendranath Bose, studying it about twenty years later, something didn't feel right. Bose, a lecturer in physics at the University of Dhaka, decided to explain the theory in his own way. He worked it out to his satisfaction by changing something crucial in the proof.

While Planck had assumed each light particle to be distinct from the other Bose took a different route. He based his approach on the idea that quantum particles behaved differently and therefore could not be described by using logic from classical physics. He considered light as a chunk of energy, with chunks of the same frequency being identical and indistinguishable from one another. This assumption effectively proved Planck's law, but had greater, far-reaching consequences, affecting all of physics as a whole.

"It was not some teacher who asked me to go and solve this little problem. I wanted to know."

An Important Step Forward

Bose didn't know it yet, but he had created a new area of physics, quantum statistics. His assumption of the indistinguishability of quanta had changed the statistical outcomes—outcomes that had real physical consequences for photons. However, journal after journal rejected his paper. Undeterred, Bose wrote to Einstein requesting his help in getting the paper published. Einstein, realizing the importance of the work, immediately submitted it for publication in the prestigious *Zeitschrift für Physik*, calling it 'an important step forward'. He also adopted Bose's idea of the indistinguishability of quanta and extended it to atoms. The two would collaborate and advance the field of quantum physics greatly.

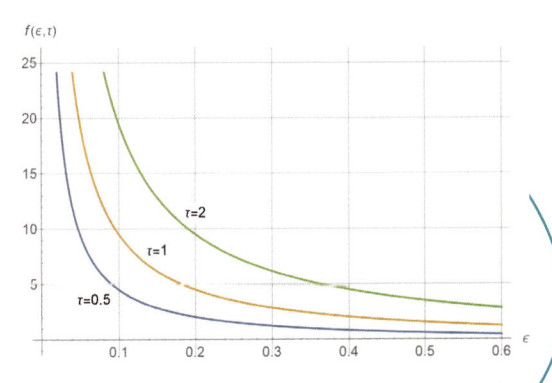

Bose Einstein distribution for three different temperatures

BOSS ON

Though Bose did not receive a Nobel for his work, he did gain immortality. The boson (a subatomic particle that obeys Bose's statistics), a fundamental element of quantum physics, is named in his honour.

53

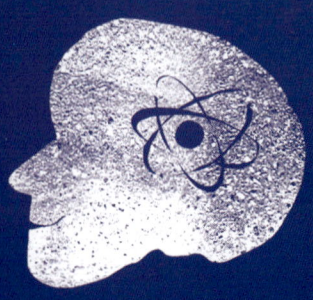

The Decoder of Protein Structure

GOPALASAMUDRAM NARAYANAN RAMACHANDRAN

8 October 1922 – 7 April 2001

Fellow, Royal Society (1977), Jawaharlal Nehru Fellow, Shanti Swarup Bhatnagar Award (1961), Ewald Prize (1991)

Ramachandran enjoyed poetry and wrote several poems on science and religion.

Created an X-Ray focusing mirror for the X-ray microscope and opened up the field of crystal topography, a technique used to analyze the structures of proteins.

> "I am admitting Ramachandran into my department as he is a bit too bright to be in yours."
> **CV RAMAN**

Though he's one of the foremost scientists of the 20th century, GN Ramachandran is not known widely outside the narrow field of molecular biophysics, the field that studies biological functions at the molecular level. He began his career as an electrical engineer at the Indian Institute of Science, Bangalore, but soon joined the physics department at the invitation of CV Raman. Raman's confidence in his protégé's genius was well placed. Ramachandran's work has shaped our understanding of the structure of proteins. It has also guided several areas of protein study, especially the design of protein-based vaccines.

- Discovered the triple helical structure of collagen, the protein that is the building block of skin, bones and muscles, with colleague Gopinath Kartha.

- Developed algorithms with colleague AV Lakshminarayana that helped to reconstruct images. This helped commercial manufacturers of x-ray tomographic scanners to build systems that could create high resolution images that were almost photographically perfect.

- Devised a general method to analyze and describe the structure of proteins along with colleagues C Ramakrishnan and V Sasisekharan. This came to be known as the Ramachandran plot.

- Set up the department of molecular biophysics at the Indian Institute of Science, Bangalore.

- His work has guided the design of protein-based vaccines.

Architect of the Indian Nuclear Programme

HOMI JEHANGIR BHABHA

30 October 1909 – 24 January 1966

Fellow, Royal Society (1941), Adams Prize (1942), Padma Bhushan (1954)

Bhabha was a fine painter and sketch artist, and some of his works are preserved in art galleries in the United Kingdom.

"The lack of proper conditions and intelligent financial support hampers the development of science in India at the pace the talent in the country would warrant."

Scientist, institution builder, artist, Homi Bhabha was a multifaceted man who pursued excellence all his life. He went to Cambridge to study engineering, but persuaded his family to let him study physics. He returned to India after a first-class degree, work experience with physicists such as Niels Bohr, Wolfgang Pauli and Enrico Fermi and fame through his vital contributions to quantum theory and cosmic radiation. Realizing that India lacked the facilities to carry out groundbreaking work in physics, he persuaded the Tata Trust to establish the Tata Institution of Fundamental Research. Dr Bhabha then established the Atomic Energy Establishment, Trombay, for multidisciplinary research (later renamed Bhabha Atomic Research Centre). Under his direction, it would become a reputed centre for excellence in science and maths. He also led India's atomic energy and nuclear power programmes, devising strategies still followed today.

- Explained phenomena such as Bhabha scattering (the path that one set of electrons and positrons take when they collide with another set) and proposed the Bhabha-Heitler Theory which describes the production of electron and positron showers in cosmic rays.

- Worked on developing nuclear weapons, on the suggestion of Prime Minister Jawaharlal Nehru.

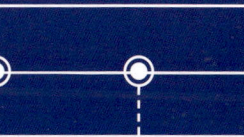

- Established the Tata Institution of Fundamental Research and the Atomic Energy Commission to further research in physics in India.

- Designed India's nuclear programme and devised the national strategy, still in use.

- Encouraged research in electronics, space science, radio astronomy and microbiology.

THE RAMAN EFFECT

Why is the sea blue?

In 1921, Sir CV Raman was on his way back to India from a trip to England. Standing on the deck of the *SS Narkunda*, he noticed that the horizon was a painting of many different blues—of the sky, the sea, the icebergs. At the time, it was believed that the sea was blue because it reflected the colours of the sky. If that was so, why were there so many shades, he wondered. Right away, Raman set about investigating the reason. By the time the ship docked at Bombay, he had a theory that the sea was blue independent of the colour of the sky. That like in the sky, the blue was the result of the scattering of sunlight through water molecules.

Sometimes, even different parts of the sea can appear to be of different colours.

The Scattering of Light

Back home in Calcutta, Raman began to study the behaviour of light when it passed through different substances. On 28 February 1928, one of his experiments showed that though light of one colour went through a liquid, it had traces of another colour when it emerged. This meant that the liquid itself was changing the colour of the light. This phenomenon of light 'scattering' into another colour when passing through

"Ask the right questions, and nature will open the doors to her secrets."
— CV Raman

58

a medium came to be known as the Raman Effect. The results of the Raman Effect (Raman-Krishnan Effect in full, after KS Krishnan, his student who helped in the study) were first published in the *Indian Journal of Physics* on 31 March 1928, and then in *Nature*. Two years later, Raman would win the Nobel for this discovery.

RAMAN'S RECORDS

Sir CV Raman was the first Asian to receive the Nobel in the Sciences. He is the only Indian Nobel laureate whose award in physics was based on work completed in India. India commemorates the day he discovered the Raman Effect, 28 February, as its National Science Day.

An Array of Applications

The Raman Effect is a quick and powerful way to identify the 'ingredients' or composition of objects. The practice of finding out what elements make up a certain material by using the Raman Effect is called Raman spectroscopy, and is applied widely in various fields. It can help identify pigments in paintings, or ceramics and gemstones in archaeology, in geology to identify minerals and their distribution, in life sciences for disease diagnosis. It is even used for security purposes, to identify explosives.

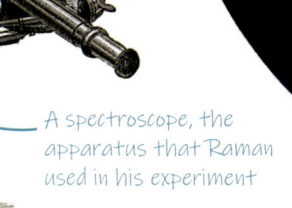

A spectroscope, the apparatus that Raman used in his experiment

The Raman Effect
Light scattering into another colour after passing through a medium

COUNTING CATS

How wildlife selfies helped give a clearer picture of tiger populations

Growing up in the 1950s, conservationist and tiger expert Ullas Karanth was enchanted by tigers. But those fabled tigers that populated local culture were on the brink of extinction. Hunting and habitat loss had nearly wiped out tigers. Over the next few decades, strict conservation laws were enacted and protected areas were created, and Project Tiger was introduced to save the species. However, their situation remained dire, with extinction remaining a real possibility.

A National Treasure

While they are charismatic creatures and should be valued solely for their own selves, as top predators, tigers have a disproportionately large impact on ecosystems. Studying them not only increases our knowledge of tigers but also indicates the health of their ecosystems. Today, India, with 20 per cent of the global tiger habitat, is home to 70 per cent of the world's tigers. The country has an even greater responsibility to ensure the survival of its national animal.

Among the earliest images of camera trapping by nature photographer George Shiras III, who pioneered the technique

Troubling Tracks

Pugmarks, traditionally used for counting tiger populations, can lead to inaccurate data. It is hard to differentiate individual tigers based on their pugmarks, and they are also notoriously long-lasting. Tigers were assumed to be flourishing in Sariska based on pugmark count, when the situation was quite the opposite. In the 90s, just as tiger poaching reached new heights, Karanth began to experiment with a new way to count tigers. While the technology had been around for some time, it had never before been put to such definite use.

FUN FACT

American ornithologist Frank M Chapman first used camera trapping to document the bird species in Barro Colorado, in Panama.

Camera trap damaged by elephants in Pakke Tiger Reserve, Karnataka

Selfies, Software and Statistics

Camera trapping uses digital cameras with sensors that can detect warm objects that move, for instance, animals. When such an animal trips the sensor, the camera records—traps—the animal's image on a hard drive. Karanth and his team ran the images from the camera through software that could identify individual tigers from the unique pattern of their stripes and then applied statistics to estimate population sizes. Though it has its limitations, camera trapping is a rigorous, reliable and accurate way to count tigers. Today, the technology is used in tandem with other methods to get a more accurate idea of their actual numbers. Camera trapping has helped shape a conservation strategy for the species

Trapping Moments
Camera traps are in use even today to observe and study animals in their natural habitat and draw quantitative as well as qualitative data.

India's Bird Man

SALIM ALI
12 November 1896 – 20 June 1987

Padma Bhushan (1958), J. Paul Getty Award for Conservation Leadership (1975) Padma Vibhushan (1976)

Salim Ali's passion for birds began with the fall of a sparrow. As a young boy who loved hunting, he shot down a bird with a yellow streak on its throat. Unable to recognize it, he went to the Bombay Natural History Society for help. There, the naturalist WS Millard identified the bird as a yellow-throated sparrow, then showed him the Society's collection of stuffed birds and lent him a few books. This incident sparked a lifelong interest in nature. Salim Ali would become a world-renowned expert on birds and the first Indian ornithologist to systematically document the birds of his country. He popularized birdwatching, communicating the beauty and wonder of nature through his writings. Several species of birds, bird sanctuaries and institutions have been named after him.

- Was the first Indian to conduct systematic bird surveys across the length and breadth of the country.

- A vocal environmental crusader, he helped establish the Bharatpur and Ranganathittu bird sanctuaries and prevent the destruction of the Silent Valley National Park.

- Emphasized the need for field observations on birds. His work on the polygamous breeding habits of the Baya Weaver was the first serious study of bird behaviour in India.

- Popularized bird watching and sparked an interest in the general public in nature through his writing.

"A monsoon ramble through the woods will delight anyone who has the eyes to see and the soul to wonder at the romance and charm of this other world within our world."

Ali once received an award of ₹5 lakhs for his work. He donated all the money to the Bombay Natural History Society.

Wrote the landmark ten-volume *Handbook of the Birds of India and Pakistan* with American ornithologist Sidney Dillon Ripley, which remains a bible for birdwatchers today.

TRADITIONAL MEDICINE

Holistic wellness systems from ancient India

India is home to several traditional medicine systems. The Ayurveda and Siddha systems were 'born' in India and practised since antiquity. About 2,000 years later, Unani medicine arrived in India from Greece, via Persia, and added to India's arsenal against diseases.

OTHER HEALING TRADITIONS
Folk and tribal medicine are also an integral part of Indian healthcare. Generally practised by communities and tribes, these cures are predominantly plant-based.

The Science of Wellbeing

Ayurveda and Siddha are best described as systems of wellness rather than healing, as they are preventive as well as curative. They also emphasize the body-mind connect, a concept that Western medicine has come to recognize relatively recently. Ayurveda is practised all over the Indian subcontinent, while Siddha is mostly confined to Tamil Nadu and adjacent areas. Both systems prescribe plant-, animal- and mineral-based medicines.

Patron Deity
Dhanvantari is considered the Hindu god of medicine and of Ayurveda.

The *Charaka Samhita* (c. 1st century CE), a foundational text of Ayurveda attributed to the physician Charaka, looks at the causes, symptoms, treatment and course of diseases. It also deals with human anatomy and functioning of the body. The *Sushruta Samhita* (7th century CE), attributed to the surgeon Sushruta, describes over 300 surgeries, many pioneering and highly advanced.

A Revival of Interest

Under the British, all indigenous medicine systems were suppressed, as they were considered inferior. After Independence, however, interest in traditional medicine systems revived. The WHO estimates that at least 70 per cent of the Indian population depends on traditional medicine. India's ministry of Ayush, which encourages research and promotion of Ayurveda, Yoga and Naturopathy, Unani, Siddha and Homoeopathy systems. Global interest in such indigenous medicine systems also sparks the hope that they will see newer advancements.

An illustrated version of the *Sushruta Samhita* written on palm leaves, dating back to the 13th century

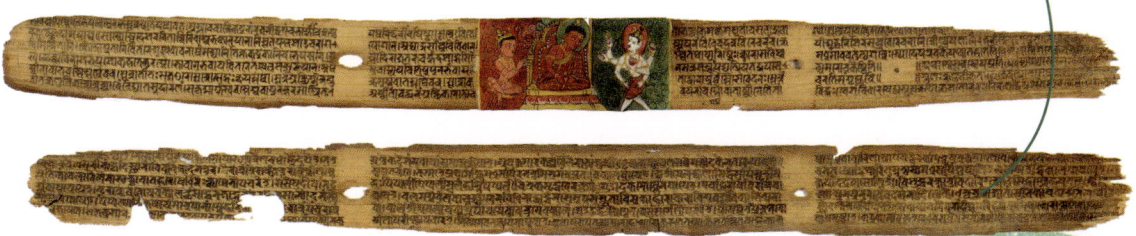

A CURE FOR KALA AZAR

How Upendranath Brahmachari saved millions of lives

"He was the Mahatma India forgot."

— Asima Chatterjee

Prior to the 19th century, little was known about the history of visceral leishmaniasis in India. The first record of the disease is from 1824, when it hit Bengal's Jessore District (now in Bangladesh) along with malaria. More popularly known as kala azar ('black fever'), it is the world's second largest parasitic killer—and one of the most dangerous yet neglected tropical diseases. It affects internal organs such as the liver, spleen and bone marrow and, if left untreated, will almost always result in death. The 1824 epidemic killed 75,000 people; over the next decades it spread through the country, turning entire villages into graveyards and earning the name kala dukh, black sorrow.

The Black Sorrow

The British, however, only took action when they realized it was affecting their workforce. They appointed Sir Ronald Ross (who had discovered that mosquitoes transmit malaria) to find a cure. Though Ross was unsuccessful, a major breakthrough came in 1903 when the disease-causing germ was identified. This opened up two lines of enquiry: how did the germ infect people, and what could treat the disease. For Upendranath Brahmachari, who had seen the terrible disease from up close in his native province of Bihar, treating the disease mattered far more. The physician set to work in a bare-bones lab in Calcutta to search for a cure.

An illustration depicting the parasites growing in various parts of the body

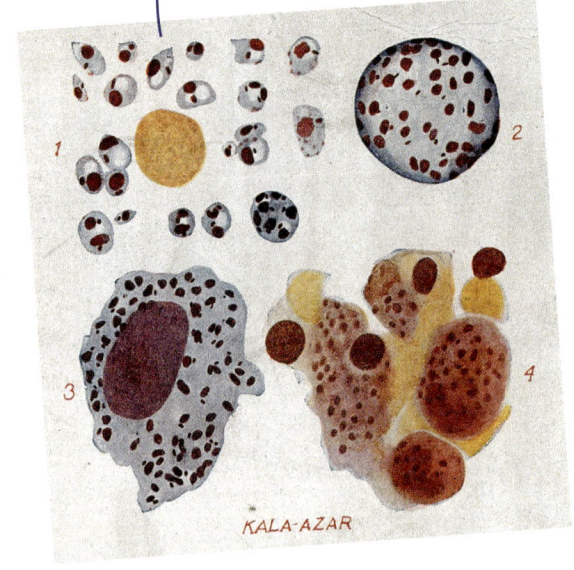

Miracle Drug

By 1910, doctors from Brazil and Italy had successfully treated a type of kala azar with tartar emetic, a form of the element antimony. But tartar emetic wasn't available in India, so Brahmachari needed to look for another cure, preferably one that was far less toxic and easier to administer. For years, he tried various options, only to find they all had significant disadvantages, until 1922, when he discovered the antimonial compound Urea Stibamine. What took over twelve weeks to cure now took barely two, and without any discomfort or intolerance. The medicine was first used on a trial basis in Assam in 1923 and on a mass scale from 1928. By 1932, close to half a million lives had been saved. The drug found immediate acceptance in Greece, France and also in China. Yet Brahmachari never patented it. He also discovered another deadly form of kala azar, Dermal Leishmanoid.

Upendranath Brahmachari died on 6 February 1946. With that, he plunged into obscurity, forgotten by the country he brought back from death's door.

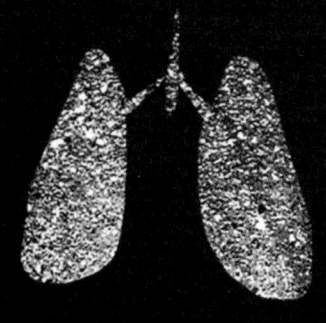

Father of Indian Pharmacology

RAM NATH CHOPRA

17 August 1882 – 13 June 1973

Knighted (1941), Companion of the Order of the Indian Empire (1934)

In his three years at Cambridge, Ram Nath Chopra earned four degrees in medicine. The world was his oyster, but he decided to come home. It was, however, a hard landing. Pharmacology, the study of drugs, was an emerging discipline. Unable to get a teaching job, he signed up with the army. It would be thirteen years before he would get the chance to live his dream. When he began his teaching career in pharmacology at Calcutta's School of Tropical Medicine in 1921, his lab barely even had chairs; by 1928, it was as well equipped as any in the UK. A one-man institution, he would pioneer systematic studies of indigenous drugs, promote Indian systems of medicine and establish himself as the father of modern Indian pharmacology.

- Set up and nurtured pharmacology as a flourishing discipline in India and helped establish laws to limit unethical practices in the industry.

- Studied various indigenous drugs like ispaghula, rauwolfia, psoralea, cobra venom and proved they have medicinal properties.

- Earned a reputation for his focus on various aspects of tropical medicine—not a subject of study for the West—as well as research on chemotherapy, clinical evaluation of drugs, drug standardization, pharmaceutical problems and diagnostic services.

- His work on traditional Indian medicines gave indigenous systems of treatment, dismissed until then as 'backward', a new lease of life and inspired many to study them.

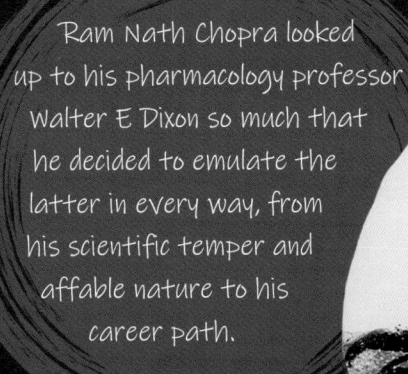

Ram Nath Chopra looked up to his pharmacology professor Walter E Dixon so much that he decided to emulate the latter in every way, from his scientific temper and affable nature to his career path.

Wrote encyclopaedic works such as the *Indigenous Drugs of India* and *Glossary of Indian Medical Plants* that are considered relevant resources even today.

THE WORLD'S VACCINE HUB
How India Made Vaccines Affordable to the World

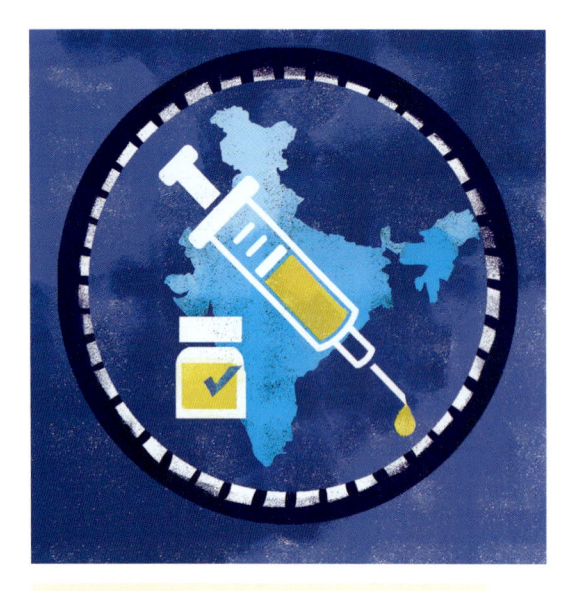

In 2020, the Covid-19 pandemic brought the world to a standstill. Countries across the world imposed lockdowns, and people battled chances of infection with isolating, social distancing and using protective equipment. Normal life could not be resumed until a large share of the world was immune to the virus. So when researchers announced that vaccines were ready, the world heaved a sigh of relief. And as the vaccine hub of the world, India had a big role to play in the global inoculation program against the coronavirus.

India's Reach
It is estimated that every second child in the world is vaccinated for measles and DPT (diphtheria, pertussis and tetanus) with Indian vaccines.

THE FIRST MODERN VACCINE

The first modern vaccine was developed by Edward Jenner in 1796, against cowpox.

The Idea

Vaccines are a form of non-disease causing bacteria and viruses that help our immune system to create cells that can destroy the actual disease causing germs when they enter our body. Vaccines began to be widely administered in the 1950s, but even forty years later, they were so expensive that people in developing countries found them unaffordable. This was about to change. In 1990, KI Varaprasad Reddy attended a WHO conference. There he learnt two things: that multinational companies priced the vaccines really high to make huge profits; and that India was considered incapable of developing vaccines. He returned home determined

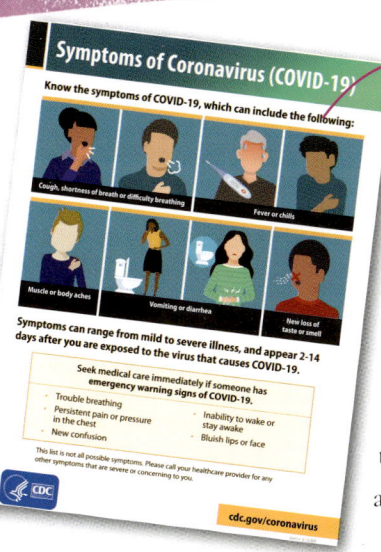

Poster describing symptoms of the infection

to produce cheap but good-quality vaccines, to make them accessible to people from all backgrounds. In 1997, his company Shantha Biotechnics released a vaccine for Hepatitis B, pricing it at $1 a dose, as against the imported vaccine, which cost $23. Fired by a similar zeal, other Indian companies developed and produced other affordable vaccines, and this brought down the prices for these vaccines globally, making them far more affordable to billions across the world.

	Country	Grant		Commercial	
		Quantity	Date of Despatch	Quantity	Date of Despatch
1	Bangladesh	33	(20) 21 Jan 21; (12) 26 Mar 21; (1) 2 Apr 2021	150.008	(50) 25 Jan 21; (20) 22 Feb 21; (10) 9 Oct 2021; (45.006) 1 Dec 2021; (25.002) 7 Dec 2021
2	Nepal	11.12	(10) 21 Jan 21; (1) 28 Mar 21; (0.12) 7 Oct 21	20	(10) 20 Feb 21; (10) 9 Oct 21
3	Iran	10	10 (BB) 8 Oct 21	1.25	(1.25 BB) 10 Mar 2021

By March 2021, India had supplied over 4.64 crore made-in-India COVID-19 vaccine doses to forty-seven countries as of March 2021.

The Impact

Today, India makes about 60 per cent of the world's vaccines. It has the capacity to produce a large variety of vaccines in huge numbers, and at relatively low costs. It's no surprise then that it played a major role in the production and development of Covid-19 vaccines. A number of countries, including Brazil, Morocco and South Africa placed orders for India's Covid-19 vaccines, while the country also sent them for free to countries such as Bhutan, Nepal, Bangladesh, the Maldives, Myanmar and Dominica as a gesture of goodwill. The impact of affordable vaccines has been felt across the world, and helped save countless lives.

NOBEL GALLERY

The Nobel, one of the most prestigious awards in the world, is given to those who, during the preceding year, have conferred the greatest benefit to humankind. Since its inception, only five Indian citizens have won the Nobel, and only one in the sciences. Here's a list of Nobel awardees and nominees in the sciences.

CV RAMAN
Winner 1930, **Physics**
For the **Raman Effect**

UPENDRANATH BRAHMACHARI
Nominated 1929, **Medicine/Physiology**
For work on **Leishmaniasis**

MEGHNAD SAHA
Nominated 1930, 1937, 1940, 1951, 1955, **Physics**
For the **Saha Equation**

NOBEL LAUREATES OF INDIAN ORIGIN

HOMI BHABHA
Nominated 1951-56, **Physics**
For Bhabha **Scattering**

SN BOSE
Nominated 1956, 1959, 1962, **Physics**
For **Bose-Einstein Statistics**

GN RAMACHANDRAN
Nominated 1964, **Physics**
For **Ramachandran Plot**

HAR GOBIND KHORANA
Physiology/Medicine, 1968
Interpretation of the genetic code
US citizen

S CHANDRASEKHAR
Physics, 1983
For theoretical studies of the physical processes of importance to the structure and evolution of the stars
US citizen

V RAMAKRISHNAN
Chemistry, 2009
For studies of the structure and function of the ribosome
Joint citizenship of the UK and US

PREMIER SCIENCE INSTITUTIONS IN INDIA

These beacons of research have brought fame and glory to the country with their findings, innovations and inventions.

Indian Institute of Science (IISC), Bengaluru
Founded in 1909, the IISC has been at the forefront of research and education in science, engineering, design and management since its inception.

National Centre for Biological Sciences (NCBS), Bengaluru
A centre of the Tata Institute of Fundamental Research, the world-renowned NCBS specializes in basic and interdisciplinary research in the frontier areas of biology.

Indian Institutes of Science Education and Research (IISER), various locations in India
These were established to provide quality education and research in basic sciences at the undergraduate level. There are currently seven such institutes across the country.

Indian Institutes of Technology (IIT), various locations in India
Every aspiring engineer's dream, the IITs offer world-class engineering programmes. There are currently twenty-three such institutes across the country.

Bhabha Atomic Research Centre (BARC), Mumbai
The country's premier nuclear research centre, BARC covers a range of areas related to nuclear science and engineering.

Indian Institute of Astrophysics (IIA), Bengaluru
This institute conducts research primarily in the areas of astronomy, astrophysics and related fields.

International Centre for Theoretical Sciences (ICTS), Bengaluru
A multi- and interdisciplinary institute that works in diverse areas such as maths, physics, biology, computer sciences and earth sciences, ICTS has been steadily gaining a reputation since its establishment in 2007.

Tata Institute of Fundamental Research (TIFR), Mumbai
Established in 1945 by Homi Bhabha, TIFR is known for its work in the natural sciences, mathematics, biological sciences and theoretical computer science.

National Institute of Immunology (NII), Delhi
This premier institute focuses on basic and applied aspects of immunity, infection, genetics, cancer, biochemistry and structural biology.

Bose Institute, Kolkata
Established by Sir JC Bose in 1917, this institute currently focuses on research in physics, chemistry, plant biology, microbiology, molecular medicine, biochemistry, biophysics, bioinformatics and environmental science.

SCIENCE ACTIVITIES

Resist this Art

You will need:

- thick white paper that can absorb some water
- white wax crayon
- paintbrushes
- small cups for the paints
- watercolour paints of your choice

Let's begin!

Using the white crayon, draw any picture you want on the paper. Press slightly hard into the paper while drawing. It might be slightly difficult to see, but don't worry about that yet.

Put the paints into the mixing tray and mix them well with water.

Now paint all over the paper using any colour that is not white, making designs as you wish. Your hidden drawing will emerge as you paint over it!

The science

When you draw with the crayon, you coat the paper with wax. When you paint over the paper with the watercolours, only those areas without wax on them will absorb the paint. The wax has formed a film over the paper that will not let the coloured water pass through—it prevents the paint from staining the paper. This is exactly how resist-dyeing works on textile.

Shadow Time

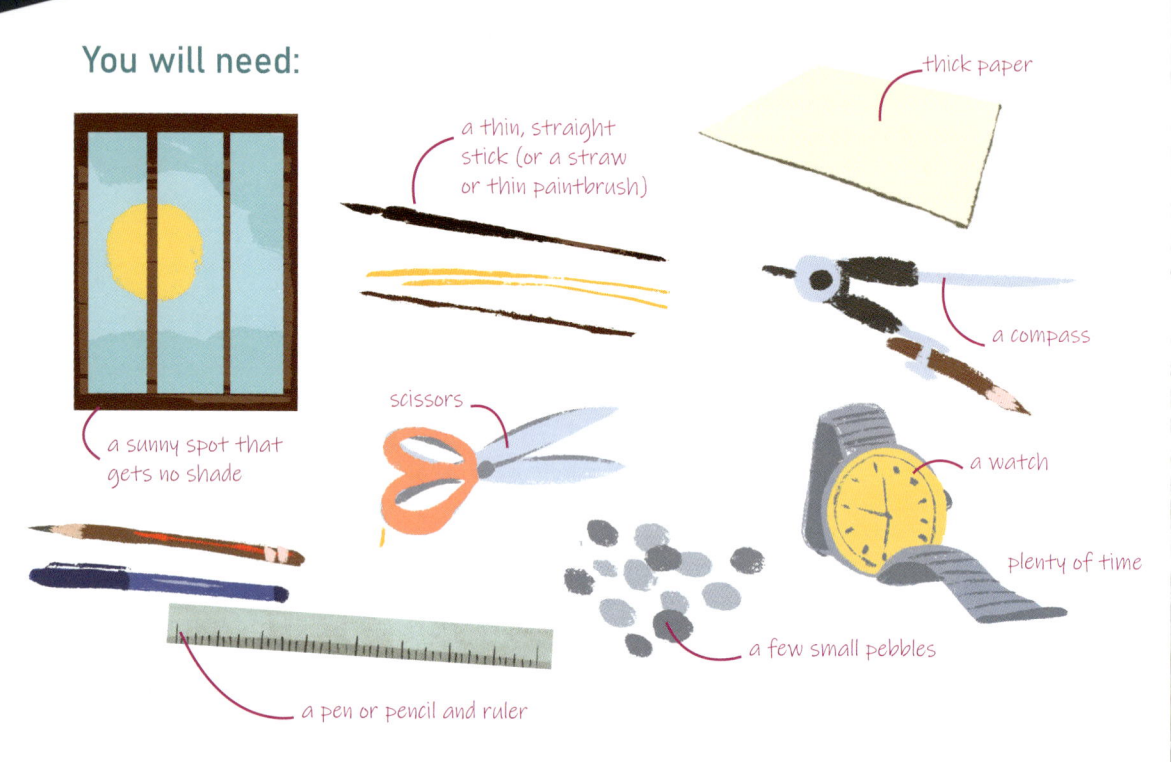

You will need:

- a sunny spot that gets no shade
- a thin, straight stick (or a straw or thin paintbrush)
- scissors
- thick paper
- a compass
- a watch
- plenty of time
- a few small pebbles
- a pen or pencil and ruler

Let's begin!

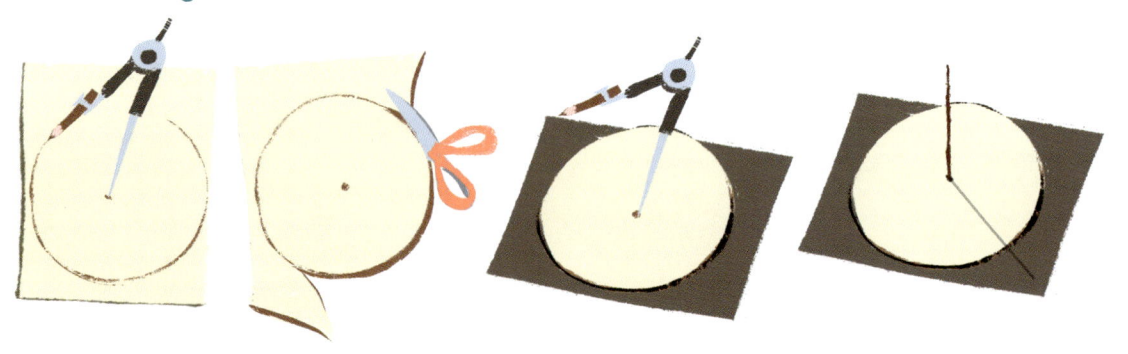

Use your compass to draw a big circle on the paper. Cut the circle out. This will act as the dial plate.

Lay it flat on the ground or any other hard surface, then poke a hole in the centre of the circle with the sharp end of the compass.

Press one end of the stick through this hole. This stick is the gnomon, the piece that casts a shadow.

78

About 10 minutes before the next full hour, take this, along with the pen, ruler, pebbles and your watch to your sunny spot. Place the sundial in the sun and weigh it down with pebbles.

Keep a close eye on the time. When the hour strikes, trace the shadow of the gnomon on the dial plate with your ruler and pen. Then write down the hour on that line.

Repeat every hour until your sundial is complete. Next time you want to tell the time, you can check it out on your sundial.

The science

The time the earth takes to rotate once on its axis is called a solar day. As the earth rotates around the sun, the shadows on earth change their position as well. By tracking the movement of the sun through the shadow it casts, we are able to accurately tell time.

Growing Germs

You will need:

- a roti or slice of bread
- 4 clean airtight jars or ziplock bags
- a cool, dark place
- a marker pen
- a helper
- patience

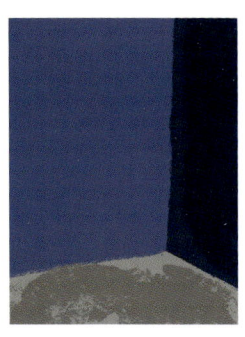

Let's begin!

Wash your hands thoroughly with soap for 20 seconds. Tear the roti or bread into 4 pieces of about the same size. They don't have to be precise.

Put one of the pieces of roti or bread into an airtight jar and label it 'Clean hands' to indicate that the roti has only touched your recently washed hands.

Rub the next piece on a regularly cleaned surface, such as your kitchen countertop. Store it in another airtight jar and label it with the name of that surface, for instance, 'Kitchen counter'.

Rub another piece of roti or bread on the floor of your house, perhaps near the entrance, where there's dust. Put it in one of the jars and label it with the name of that surface, such as 'Living room floor'.

For the last piece, ask someone with unwashed hands to put it into the last jar. Label that 'Unwashed hands'.

Store these jars in a cool, dark area for about a week. Then go back and check. They will all have mouldy growth! Which has the most and which the least?

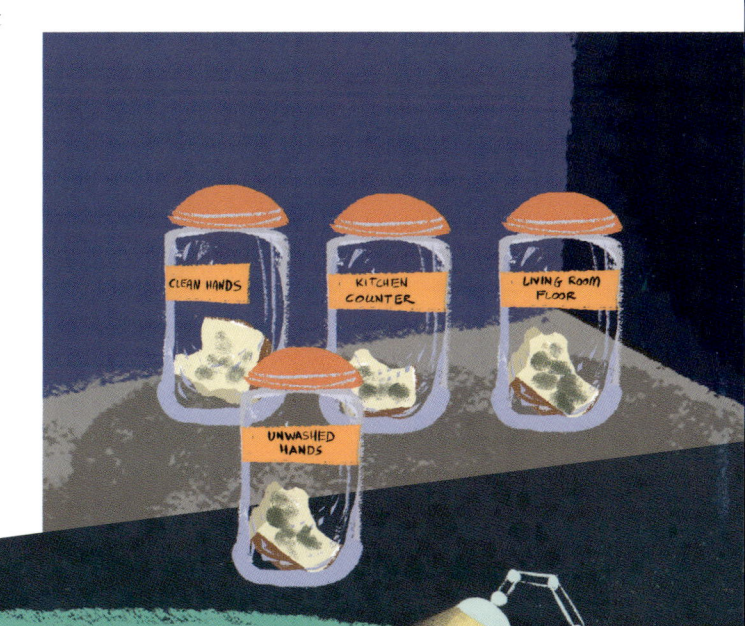

The science

All three of the roti or bread pieces have ended up with white, black or blue-green fuzz. You can see it now because it has grown over the week to become large enough to be visible. The dirtiest piece has the most germs, while the one you handled with clean hands has the least. Germs are all around us, even though we can't see them. Two of the most common germs are bacteria and viruses. While some germs, such as the bacteria that live in our gut, are good for us, others can cause infections. Yet others are used to make medicines such as penicillin, which comes from mould, and kills many harmful bacteria. Vaccines are a form of germs that are introduced into our body. They teach the body's immune system to recognize the germ as an enemy and build defences against it. So when your body is actually attacked, it is well prepared and can fight off the infection.

IMAGE CREDITS

ASTRONOMY
Jantar Mantar: Wikimedia Commons; Author: Jakub Hałun; https://commons.wikimedia.org/wiki/File:20191218_Rashivilaya_Yantra,_Jantar_Mantar,_Jaipur,_0908_8986.jpg

Mysore Rockets
Tipu Sultan: Wikimedia Commons; Author: Unknown; Source: Kate Brittlebank, *Tipu Sultan's Search for Legitimacy*, New Delhi: Oxford University Press, 1997; https://commons.wikimedia.org/wiki/File:TipuSultan1790.jpg

Battle of Guntur: Wikimedia Commons; Author: Charles H. Hubbell; Source: nasa.gov; https://commons.wikimedia.org/wiki/File:Rocket_warfare.jpg

BOTANY
Cork under the microscope: Wikimedia Commons; Author: Robert Hooke; https://commons.wikimedia.org/wiki/File:Cork_Micrographia_Hooke.png

MADE IN INDIA
Flush toilet: Wikimedia Commons; Author: Ladarozan; https://commons.wikimedia.org/wiki/File:Wc1.jpg

Cotton fabric: Wikimedia Commons; Author: The Board of Trustees of the Science Museum; Source: https://collection.sciencemuseumgroup.org.uk/objects/co8412601; https://commons.wikimedia.org/wiki/File:Chintz_palampore_India_18th_century.jpg

Akbar's Gulalbar: Wikimedia Commons; Author: Unknown; Source: *The Akbarnama*; https://commons.wikimedia.org/wiki/File:AkbarHunt.jpg

Ink and Paper
Manuscript: Wikimedia Commons; Author: Manoj Choudhury; https://commons.wikimedia.org/wiki/File:Odia_palm_leaf_manuscript.JPG
Statue of Goddess Saraswati: Wikimedia Commons; Author: Unknown; Source: Walter's Art Museum; https://commons.wikimedia.org/wiki/File:Indian_-_Sarasvati_-_Walters_2550.jpg

Shampoo
Sheikh Din Muhammad: Wikimedia Commons; Author: Thomas Mann Baynes; Source: https://dams-brightonmuseums.org.uk/assetbank-pavilion/action/viewAsset?id=11198; https://commons.wikimedia.org/wiki/File:Sake_Dean_Mahomed.jpg

Indian Gooseberry: Wikimedia Commons; Author: Maniv34; https://commons.wikimedia.org/wiki/File:Indian_Gooseberries_ripe.JPG

Dyes and Mordants
Priest king from Indus Valley: Wikimedia Commons; Author: Mamoon Mengal; Source: World66; https://en.wikipedia.org/wiki/File:Mohenjo-daro_Priesterk%C3%B6nig.jpeg

Indigo plant: Wikimedia Commons; Author: Unknown; Source: Wellcome Images; https://commons.wikimedia.org/wiki/File:Indigo_plant_(Indigofera_tinctoria_L.),_flowering_stem_with_Wellcome_V0042997EL.jpg

Person block printing: Wikimedia Commons; Author: Anne Roberts; Source: Flickr; https://commons.wikimedia.org/wiki/File:Woman_doing_Block_Printing_at_Halasur_village,_Karnataka.jpg

METALLURGY
Emperor Jahangir: Wikimedia Commons; Author: Abu al-Hasan; Source: https://images1.bonhams.com/erez4/erez?src=Images/live/2011-01/21/8242176-1-6.jpg; https://commons.wikimedia.org/wiki/File:Jahangir_-_Abu_al-Hasan.jpeg

QUANTUM PHYSICS
Bose-Einstein distribution: Wikimedia Commons; Author: Avivorly; https://commons.wikimedia.org/wiki/File:Bose_Einstein_distribution.jpg

The Raman Effect
Waters of the sea: Wikimedia Commons; Author: dronepicr; Source: Flickr; https://commons.wikimedia.org/wiki/File:Aerial_view_of_the_Sea_of_Crete_at_Kleftiko_on_Milos_Island,_Greece.jpg

Spectroscope: Wikimedia Commons; Author: Unknown; Source: John Browning, *How to Work With the Spectroscope*, 1878; https://commons.wikimedia.org/wiki/File:Solar_Automatic_Spectroscope.png

COUNTING CATS
Damaged camera trap: Wikimedia Commons; Author: Nandini Velho; https://en.wikipedia.org/wiki/File:Camera_trap_damaged_by_elephants_in_Pakke_Tiger_Reserve.JPG

Deer: Wikimedia Commons; Author: George Shiras III; Source: National Geographic; https://commons.wikimedia.org/wiki/File:Two_deer_in_the_woods_at_night,_by_George_Shiras_III.jpg

TRADITIONAL MEDICINE
Dhanvantari: Wikimedia Commons; Author: HP Nadig; https://commons.wikimedia.org/wiki/File:Dhanvantari-at-Ayurveda-expo.jpg

Sushruta Samhita: Wikimedia Commons: Author: Unknown; Source: Los Angeles County Museum of Art; https://commons.wikimedia.org/wiki/File:The_Susruta-Samhita_or_Sahottara-Tantra_(A_Treatise_on_Ayurvedic_Medicine)_LACMA_M.87.271a-g_(1_of_8).jpg

Kala Azar
Parasites: Wikimedia Commons; Author: Unknown; Source: Wellcome Images; https://commons.wikimedia.org/wiki/File:Parasites_of_the_tropical_diseases_Kala-Azar_and_Oriental_So_Wellcome_V0022616.jpg

The World's Vaccine Hub
Symptoms of Covid: Wikimedia Commons; Author: US Centers for Disease Control and Prevention; Source: cdc.gov; https://commons.wikimedia.org/wiki/File:Symptoms_of_COVID-19_(English).pdf

INDIA AT THE OLYMPICS

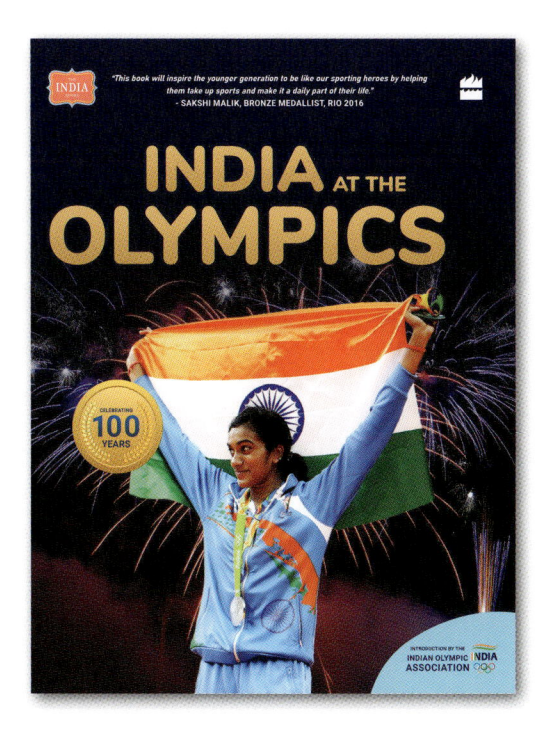

India at the Olympics celebrates 100 years of Indian athletes' participation in the world's biggest sporting event.

Packed with rare images and colourful illustrations, this unique book:
- Traces the incredible history of the Olympics from the time of the Ancient Greek Olympics to its present, modern-day avatar
- Focuses on India's 100-year participation – its achievements and records
- Includes profiles of India's biggest sporting legends such as Dhyan Chand, PT Usha, Karnam Malleswari, Saina Nehwal, PV Sindhu, Mary Kom, Abhinav Bindra and Leander Paes among others

A visual treat for sports enthusiasts of all ages!

INCREDIBLE INDIANS

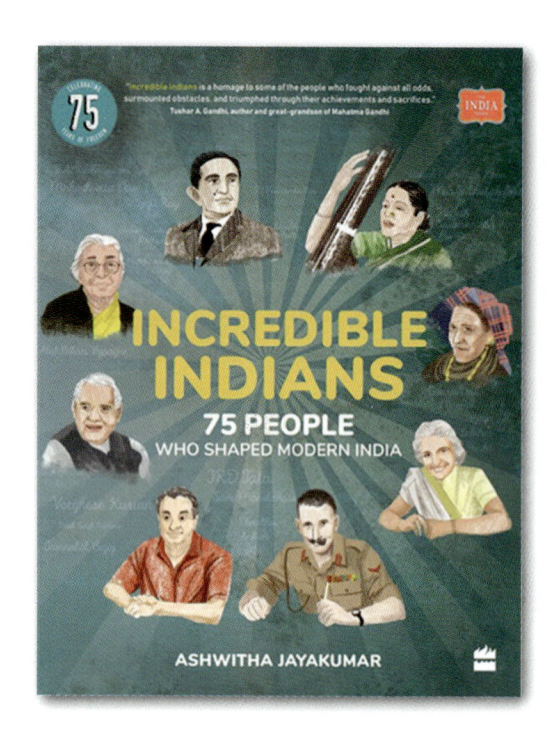

From some of the best-known icons of the nationalist movement to political leaders, scientists and public servants who laid the foundations of the new nation; from artists and writers who epitomized India's diversity and cultural variety to activists who fought for the rights of the most vulnerable, this book is an excellent introduction to the history of the modern Indian nation.

This book includes:
- Concise biographies of political figures, activists, environmentalists, artists, writers and industrialists
- Detailed historical and social background to the making of modern India
- Trivia and facts about the lives and achievements of eminent Indians

Incredible Indians is a homage to the fascinating individuals who helped build India as we know it today.

INDIA IN SPACE

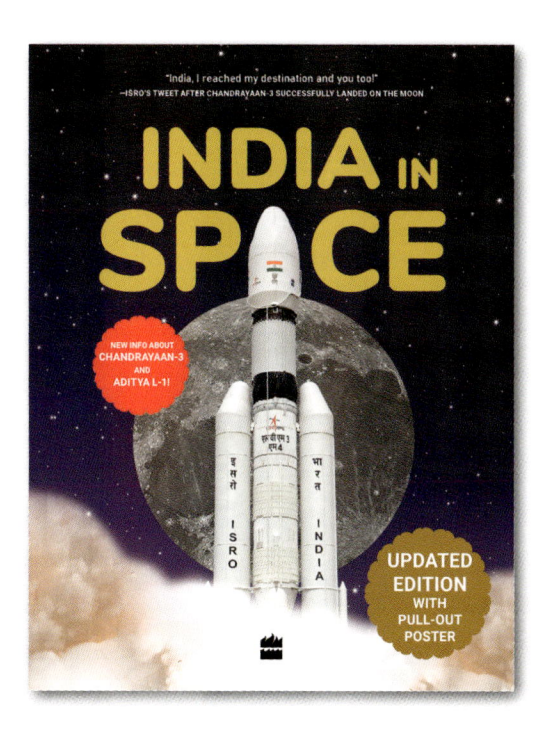

As we rocket into space on the back of several successful missions, this book examines India's glorious space trajectory starting from its first venture, the Aryabhata, to its most recent mission to the Moon, Chandrayaan-3, along with India's collaboration with international space agencies.
Presented through crisp stories and timelines accompanied by stunning pictures, this brilliantly designed, information-rich book will give you a complete update on India's unique place in the world of space exploration.

This book also includes:
- Space trivia, timeline of the Indian space programme and milestones of other spacefaring nations
- Valuable tips on space careers and scholarships for aspiring astronauts, space scientists and explorers
- Exciting activities by NASA

Pick up this book to explore India's incredible journey into space!